C000039581

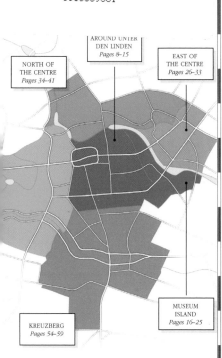

EYEWITNESS TRAVEL

BERLIN

POCKET
GUIDE

LONDON, NEW YORK,
MELBOURNE, MUNICH AND DELHI
www.dk.com

This edition produced by Silva Editions Ltd.,
233 Woodcote Road, Purley, Surrey CR8 3PB

PROJECT EDITOR Sylvia Goulding

ART EDITOR Paula Keogh

COPY EDITOR Gisela Roberts

RESEARCH AND INDEX Mike Goulding

CARTOGRAPHER John Plumer

Conceived by Redback Publishing,
25 Longhope Drive, Farnham, Surrey GU10 4SN.

Printed and bound by Leo Paper Products Ltd.

First published in the UK in 2007
by Dorling Kindersley Limited
80 Strand, London WC2R 0RL

15 16 17 18 10 9 8 7 6 5 4 3 2 1

Copyright 2007, 2015 © Dorling Kindersley Limited, London
A Penguin Random House Company

Reprinted with revisions 2009, 2011, 2013, 2015

MIX
Paper from
responsible sources
FSC
www.fsc.org   FSC™ C018179

**The information in this
DK Eyewitness Travel Guide is checked regularly.**
Every effort has been made to ensure that this book is as up-to-date as
possible at the time of going to press. Some details, however, such as
telephone numbers, opening hours, prices, gallery hanging
arrangements and travel information, are liable to change. The
publishers cannot accept responsibility for any consequences arising
from the use of this book, nor for any material on third-party websites,
and cannot guarantee that any website address in this book will be a
suitable source of travel information. We value the views and
suggestions of our readers highly. Please write to:
Publisher, DK Eyewitness Travel Guides, Dorling Kindersley,
80 Strand, London WC2R 0RL, UK, or email: travelguides@dk.com.

The old and new Kaiser-Wilhelm-Gedächtniskirche

CONTENTS

The Berlin bear

Central Berlin

The city's historic core lies in Unter den Linden and Museum Island. West of the centre is the Tiergarten. To the south is Kreuzberg, known for its alternative lifestyle. Further west is Kurfürstendamm, centre of former West Berlin. At its edge is the old royal palace, Schloss Charlottenburg.

Kulturforum
This collection of museums and libraries is also home to the Berlin Philharmonic (see p44).

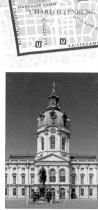

Schloss Charlottenburg
The historic rooms of the former Hohenzollern summer palace invite visitors to experience a slice of Prussian history, while the Baroque-style gardens are among the most beautiful in Germany (see pp70–71).

0 km   1

0 mile   1

KEY

🚉 Railway station

Ⓤ U-Bahn

Ⓢ S-Bahn

Berliner Dom
With its black marble staircase and towering dome, this neo-Renaissance cathedral is Berlin's largest and most lavish church (see pp20–21).

Rotes Rathaus
Designed to resemble an Italian Renaissance palazzo, Berlin's town hall is the office of the Governing Mayor and the political centre of power in Greater Berlin (see p28).

Berlin's Highlights

Berlin is one of the most fascinating capitals in the world. You'll find no other place where art and culture, museums and theatres, entertainment and nightlife are more diverse and exciting than in this vibrant city on the banks of the Spree river.

Jüdisches Museum in Kreuzberg

Museums and Galleries

Gemäldegalerie
This world-famous art collection houses European paintings from the 13th to the 19th centuries (*see p47*).

Neues Museum
Reconstructed by David Chipperfield Architects in 2009, this museum's most famous exhibit is the limestone bust of Egyptian Queen Nefertiti (*see p19*).

Pergamonmuseum
Brimming with treasures from ancient times, this museum has the look and feel of a Babylonian vault (*see p22*).

Jüdisches Museum
Housed in a building by Daniel Libeskind, this museum illustrates the history and culture of Germany's Jewish community (*see pp56–7*).

Altes Museum
This beautiful Neo-Classical building houses Greek and Roman antiquities as well as a unique collection of Egyptian artifacts (*see p19*).

Historic Buildings

Schloss Bellevue
Philipp Daniel Boumann's Neo-Classical palace was carefully restored after bomb damage during World War II (*see p52*).

Brandenburger Tor
One of 18 original city gates, the Brandenburg Gate has come to be the main symbol of Berlin (*see p14*).

Zeughaus
Designed by J A Nering and others and built in 1695–1730 as Berlin's first Baroque building, the former royal arsenal is now the Deutsches Historisches Museum, with additions by I M Pei (*see p10*).

Berliner Dom
The huge Neo-Baroque Berlin Cathedral has a grand interior designed by Julius Raschdorff in 1894–1905 (*see pp20–21*).

Reichstag
Built in 1884–94 by Paul Wallot to house the German parliament, the Reichstag has a glass dome added by Norman Foster (*see p53*).

The Reichstag, with modern dome

The hypermodern Sony Center

Modern Architecture

Bauhaus-Archiv
Designed by Walter Gropius (1883–1969), this Cubist structure was completed in 1978 and houses the Bauhaus-Museum (see p48).

Kammermusiksaal
The chamber music hall was designed by Hans Scharoun and built in 1984–7 by his pupil, Edgar Wisniewski (see p44).

Sony Center
One of Berlin's most exciting architectural complexes, this was built in 1996–2000 by Helmut Jahn. Its piazza remains a highly popular attraction (see p51).

Haus der Kulturen der Welt
The House of World Cultures was designed by Hugh Stubbins and built in 1956–7 as a congress hall. Rebuilt following its partial collapse, it reopened in 1989 as a culture centre and is now famous for its jazz festivals (see p52).

Neue Nationalgalerie
Designed by Mies van der Rohe and built in 1965–8, this gallery was based on earlier designs for the Havana headquarters of Bacardi (see p45).

Parks and Gardens

Schlosspark Charlottenburg
Among the most beautiful in all Germany, the smaller garden has a French-style Baroque design, while the larger area is an English-style park (see p71).

Tiergarten
Once a hunting reserve, this central park is Berlin's largest green space. It was landscaped in the 1830s by Peter Lenné (see p49).

Viktoriapark
The old municipal park is today one of Berlin's most popular green spaces. At its highest point stands a monument to the Prussian victory over Napoleon (see p59).

Zoologischer Garten
This zoo in the centre of the city, dating from 1844, boasts some 18,000 animals, including animal celebrities such as silverback gorilla Ivo (see p62).

Monbijoupark
This small park once surrounded Monbijou Palace. It features a marble bust of the German writer and naturalist Chamisso (see p37).

Viktoriapark in Kreuzberg

UNTER DEN LINDEN

The area around Unter den Linden is among the most attractive in Berlin. Its growth started during the Baroque period and despite bombing in World War II and only partial rebuilding by the East German government, it still has the highest concentration of historic buildings in Berlin.

SIGHTS AT A GLANCE

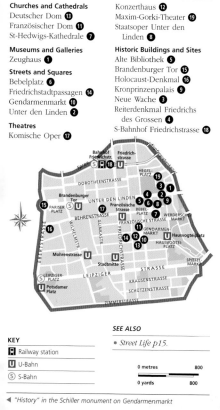

KEY

🚉 Railway station

Ⓤ U-Bahn

Ⓢ S-Bahn

| 0 metres | | 800 |
| 0 yards | | 800 |

◀ "History" in the Schiller monument on Gendarmenmarkt

Unter den Linden, a grand avenue lined by lime trees

Zeughaus (Deutsches Historisches Museum) ❶

Map H3. Unter den Linden 2. Open daily. Adm charge.

Originally the royal arsenal, the Zeughaus was built in 1695–1730 from plans by Johann Arnold Nering. It is an impressive Baroque structure, with its main and side wings surrounding a central courtyard that is protected by a modern glass cupola roof. Of special note are Andreas Schlüter's figures of 22 dying warriors, lining the arcades in the courtyard. They vividly portray the horrors of war. A cone-shaped glass annexe, designed and erected by the Chinese-born architect I M Pei in 2001 for special and temporary shows, lies behind the museum.

The permanent exhibition includes a collection entitled "German History in Images and Artifacts from Two Millennia". The exhibits date from the early medieval German Empire through the Reformation and the Thirty Years' War, the wars of Liberation and the failed 1848 Revolution, right up to the two World Wars and other events of the 20th century.

Unter den Linden ❷

Map G4.

This magnificent avenue, originally a royal route from the king's town dwelling to the Tiergarten, became Berlin's main street in the 18th century. Today, the old buildings have been restored and modern architecture has created new highlights.

Neue Wache ❸

Map H3. Unter den Linden 4. Open daily. Free.

This Neo-Classical structure by Karl Friedrich Schinkel is now Germany's Central Memorial for the Victims of War and Tyranny. Käthe Kollwitz's *Pietà* sculpture stands in the centre.

Façade of the Zeughaus

Frederick the Great's statue

Reiterdenkmal Friedrichs des Grossen ❹

Map H4. Unter den Linden.

This massive bronze statue, 5.6 m (18.5 ft) tall, stands on the central reservation of Unter den Linden. Designed by Christian Daniel Rauch – a pupil of Johann Gottfried Schadow – and created in 1839–51, it depicts Frederick the Great on horseback. At the base of the statue stand Frederick's generals in the front, and great intellectuals of the day at the back.

Alte Bibliothek ❺

Map H4. Bebelplatz.

One of Berlin's great Baroque buildings, the Old Library was built in 1775 by Georg Christian Unger to house the royal library collection. His design was based on an earlier plan by Fischer von Erlach for the Vienna Hofburg. The building now houses Humboldt University's law faculty.

Alte Bibliothek on Bebelplatz

Bebelplatz ❻

Map H4.

Once named Opernplatz (Opera Square), this wide open space was designed by Georg von Knobelsdorff as the focal point of his Forum Fridericianum, recalling the glories of ancient Rome. A translucent panel with empty bookshelves below created by Micha Ullman in 1995 commemorates the infamous Nazi book burning which took place here in 1933.

St-Hedwigs-Kathedrale

St-Hedwigs-Kathedrale ❼

Map H4. Bebelplatz. Open daily. Services Sat and Sun. Free.

This huge church, set back from the road and crowned with a dome, is the Catholic Cathedral of the Roman Archdiocese of Berlin. It was built to serve the Catholics of Silesia, part of present-day Poland, which became part of the Kingdom of Prussia in 1742 following defeat in the Silesian Wars of 1740–63. Designed by Georg W von Knobelsdorff, it was built in 1747–78, with additional work in 1886–7. After damage during World War II it was rebuilt in 1952–63. The crypt holds the tombs of many bishops of Berlin, a 16th-century Madonna and a Pietà dating from 1420.

The Neo-Classical façade of the Kronprinzenpalais

Staatsoper Unter den Linden ❽

Map H4. Unter den Linden 7.
Closed for renovations until 2016.

The State Opera House's early Neo-Classical façade is one of the most beautiful sights on Unter den Linden. It was built by Georg W von Knobelsdorff in 1741–3. After a fire, it was restored in 1843–4 by Carl Ferdinand Langhans, who altered only its interior. After wartime destruction, the opera house was almost completely rebuilt in 1952–5; it is currently undergoing a major restoration that will last until 2016. It has hosted famous singers, musicians and artists; one of its directors and conductors was Richard Strauss. The current conductor and director is Daniel Barenboim.

Ornamentation on the Staatsoper

Kronprinzenpalais ❾

Map H4. Unter den Linden 3.
Open only for exhibitions.

This late Neo-Classical palace was originally a modest house dating from 1663–9. Philipp Gerlach added extensions in 1732–3, and Johann Heinrich Strack added a storey in 1856–7. The palace served the royal family until the end of the monarchy. In 1919–37, the Nationalgalerie was based here. Under Communist rule it was reserved for official government guests. It was here, in August 1990, that the pact was signed paving the way for reunification.

Gendarmenmarkt ❿

Map H4.

This is one of Berlin's most beautiful squares, created at the end of the 17th century as a market square for the new Friedrichstadt. It is named after the Regiment Gens d'Armes who had their stables here, and is reminiscent of an Italian piazza. In 1950 it was renamed Platz der Akademie, but after reunification the square reverted to its original name.

Französischer Dom, the French cathedral

Französischer Dom ⑪

Map H4. Gendarmenmarkt 5. Open Tue–Sun. Adm charge.

One of two churches on the opposite sides of Konzerthaus, the French cathedral was built for the Huguenot community, who found refuge in Protestant Berlin following their expulsion from France after the revocation of the Edict of Nantes. The modest church, built in 1701–5 by Louis Cayart and Abraham Quesnay, was based on a Huguenot church in Charenton, France. The main entrance, on the west side (facing Charlottenstrasse), leads to a simple interior. It features a late-Baroque organ from 1754.

The structure is dominated by a huge cylindrical tower, ringed by Corinthian porticoes at its base. Tower and porticoes were designed by Carl von Gontard and added c.1785. The Dom houses the Huguenot Museum, which traces the history of the Huguenots in France and Brandenburg. They played a crucial part in the rise of Berlin as a city of commerce.

Konzerthaus ⑫

Map G4. Gendarmenmarkt 2. Open most days.

Home of the Berlin Symphony Orchestra and formerly known as the Schauspielhaus, Karl Friedrich Schinkel's Concert Hall was built in 1818–21. After World War II, it was reconstructed with a different interior layout and the exterior was restored to its former glory.

Konzerthaus

Deutscher Dom ⑬

Map H3. Gendarmenmarkt 1. Open Tue–Sun. Free.

The German cathedral, on the south side of the square, is an old German Protestant-Reformed church. Designed by Martin Grünberg, it was built in 1708 by Giovanni Simonetti. In 1785 a dome-covered tower was added, identical to that of the Französischer Dom. Burned down in 1945, the church was rebuilt in 1993.

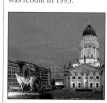

Deutscher Dom façade

Brandenburger Tor, once a symbol of the divided city

Friedrichstadtpassagen 14

Map G4. Friedrichstrasse
Quartiers 205, 206, 207. Free.

These passages are part of a huge development of luxury commercial and residential buildings erected in the 1990s along Friedrichstrasse. Quartier 207 is the famous French department store Galeries Lafayette, occupying a building designed by Jean Nouvel and made mostly of glass. The next passage, Quartier 206, the work of the American design team Pei Cobb Freed & Partners, has offices and luxury boutiques. The southernmost building in the complex, and the largest passage, is Quartier 205, which is the work of Oswald Mathias Ungers.

Brandenburger Tor 15

Map G4. Pariser Platz.

The Brandenburg Gate is the quintessential symbol of Berlin. Since its restoration in 2002, this magnificent Neo-Classical structure is now lit up more brightly than ever. Built by Carl G Langhans in 1789–91 and modelled on the entrance to the Acropolis in ancient Athens, the Gate has, since the 19th century, been the backdrop for many events in the city's turbulent history. The gate is topped by the 6-m- (20-ft-) high Quadriga, created in 1794 by Schadow, who used his niece as a model for the goddess of Victory driving her chariot. Until reunification in 1990 the gate stood in East Berlin.

Holocaust-Denkmal 16

Map G4. Ebertstrasse.
Open Tue–Sun. Free.

In 2005 a memorial for the Jews killed by the Nazis in 1933–45 was finished. The work of US architect Peter Eisenmann, it covers 19,000 sq m (205,000 sq ft) near the Brandenburg Gate. Above ground, a field of concrete slabs symbolizes the murdered millions; beneath lies an information centre.

Komische Oper ⓱

Map G4. Behrenstrasse 55–7.
Ticket charge.

The modern façade of this theatre hides one of Berlin's most impressive interiors. Built in 1892 by Fellner and Helmer, it has been a variety theatre and the German National Theatre in the past, only housing the Komische Oper since World War II.

Maxim-Gorki-Theater

S-Bahnhof Friedrichstrasse ⓲

Map G3. Friedrichstrasse.

Bahnhof Friedrichstrasse used to be the S-Bahn border station between East and West Berlin. Built in 1882 by Johannes Vollmer, it was given a roof in 1925. Much of the original no longer exists, but there is a model at the Stasi-Museum.

Maxim-Gorki-Theater ⓳

Map H3. Am Festungsgraben 2.

Berlin's oldest concert hall, built in 1827, was once a singing school. It has played host to many famous composers and musicians, such as violinist Niccolò Paganini and pianist Franz Liszt. Today it is a modern drama theatre.

STREET LIFE

RESTAURANTS

Brasserie am Gendarmenmarkt
Map H4. Taubenstrasse 30.
Tel 20 45 35 01. **Expensive**
Quality brasserie food and great steaks, in one of Berlin's most attractive squares. Superb Art Deco interior.

Dressler
Map G4. Unter den Linden 39.
Tel 204 44 22. **Moderate**
Perfect for dining before or after visiting the theatre. Traditional French and German fare.

Grill Royal
Map G3. Friedrichstrasse 105b.
Tel 28 87 92 88. **Expensive**
Chic waterfront restaurant attracting stars and celebrities. Reserve well in advance.

BARS AND PUBS

Lutter & Wegner
Map G4. Charlottenstrasse 56.
Pleasant wine bar with a German-Austrian bias.

Newton-Bar
Map G4. Charlottenstrasse 57.
This elegant bar serves the best cocktails in town.

SHOPPING

Berlin Story
Map G4. Unter den Linden 40.
This bookshop/café/museum has everything on Berlin, from books to marble busts.

Galeries Lafayette
Map G4. Friedrichstrasse 76–8.
Elegant fashion and gourmet food in this French store.

See p80 for price codes.

MUSEUM ISLAND

A museum complex of international importance, this island was inhabited from the 13th century and later housed an imperial palace, which was destroyed in 1950. Some interesting buildings remain, including the huge Berliner Dom and the impressive collection of museums that give the island its name – Museumsinsel.

SIGHTS AT A GLANCE

Museums and Galleries

Alte Nationalgalerie **7**
Altes Museum **5**
Bodemuseum **9**
Märkisches Museum **12**
Neues Museum **6**
Pergamonmuseum **8**

Streets, Squares and Parks

Lustgarten **4**
Märkisches Ufer **13**
Schlossplatz **1**

Historic Buildings

Berliner Dom pp20–21 **3**
Ermeler-Haus **14**
Gertraudenbrücke **15**
Marstall **10**
Nicolai-Haus **16**
Ribbeckhaus **11**
Schlossbrücke **2**

SEE ALSO

● *Street Life p25.*

KEY	
🚌	Bus terminus
Ⓤ	U-Bahn
Ⓢ	S-Bahn

0 metres	600
0 yards	600

◀ *The elegant Bodemuseum, with the Fernsehturm in the background*

Schlossplatz ❶

Map H4.

This huge square is lorded over by the Humboldt-Box, a sleek, four-storey information-centre devoted to the history of the Berliner Stadtschloss (City Palace), the main residence of the Hohenzollerns for almost 500 years. In 1950–51, the palace was demolished under the GDR, but is now being reconstructed, with work scheduled until 2019.

Schlossplatz, first built in 1451

Schlossbrücke ❷

Map H3/4.

This is one of the town's most beautiful bridges, connecting Schlossplatz with Unter den Linden. It was built in 1824 to a design by Karl Friedrich Schinkel, one of Germany's most influential architects. Statues were added to the bridge's granite pillars in 1853. These figures were also created by Schinkel, and are made from stunning white Carrara marble. They depict scenes from Greek mythology. The wrought-iron balustrade is decorated with intertwined sea creatures.

Berliner Dom ❸

See pp20–21.

Lustgarten ❹

Map H3.

The enchanting Pleasure Garden in front of the Altes Museum grew kitchen produce for the Stadtschloss until the late 16th century. Statuary and exotic plants were added in the reign of the Great Elector, but Friedrich Wilhelm I (1688–1740) turned it into an army drill ground. After the Altes Museum was built in 1830, it became a park, designed by Lenné. Its present restoration is based on Lenné's designs.

Altes Museum ❺

Map H3. Am Lustgarten (Bodestrasse 1–3). Open daily. Adm charge.

The museum building, by Karl Friedrich Schinkel, is a beautiful Neo-Classical structure, with an impressive 87-m- (285-ft-) high portico supported by 18 Ionic columns, behind which the shiny red imitation marble used in its construction is visible. Officially opened in

Marble statues on Schlossbrücke

The portico and Ionic columns of the Altes Museum

1830, this was one of the first purpose-built museums in Europe, constructed to house the royal collection of paintings and antiquities. Since 1998 Altes Museum has housed parts of the Antikensammlung, a magnificent collection of Greek and Roman artifacts.

Neues Museum

Map H3. Bodestrasse 1–3. Open daily. Adm charge.

The Neues Museum was built in the mid-1800s and badly damaged in World War II. Following a stunning reconstruction under the direction of British architect David Chipperfield, the Neues Museum once again houses a remarkable collection of Egyptian art, as well as artifacts from ancient Troy.

The highlight of the Neues Museum's Egyptian section is the fascinating collection from 19th-century archaeological digs in Tell el-Amarna, the capital of Egypt during the era of the reign of Amenhotep IV.

The most delightful exhibit is the delicate, long-necked bust of Nefertiti, carved from limestone. It was discovered in 1912, in the workshop of the sculptor Thutmosis.

Alte Nationalgalerie 7

Map H3. Bodestrasse 1–3. Open Tue–Sun. Adm charge.

The Old National Gallery, built in 1866–76 to designs by Friedrich August Stüler, stands on a high platform. The gallery is topped with an equestrian statue of Friedrich Wilhelm IV and the façade of the building is preceded by a magnificent colonnade. The collection includes works by Wilhelm Leibl, Max Liebermann, Adolph von Menzel and Arnold Böcklin as well as paintings by the French Impressionists. The gallery also owns one of Germany's largest collections of 19th-century sculptures. Two exhibition halls are devoted to the German Romantic era and works by Caspar David Friedrich, Karl Friedrich Schinkel and Karl Blechen.

Berliner Dom ③

Berlin Cathedral, the largest and most lavish church in the city, was reopened in 1993 after almost 40 years of restoration. Built in 1747–50, the building has a grandeur that reflects the aspirations to power of Germany's then ruling Hohenzollern dynasty.

Royal crest of Friedrich III

The Church Interior *was designed by Julius Raschdorff at the start of the 20th century. Ornate in style, it has been largely restored to its former glory.*

Figures of the apostles

Philipp der Grossmütige *(the Magnanimous) is commemorated by this Walter Schott statue at the base of the arcade.*

Main entrance

The Hohenzollern Sarcophagi *are laid out in the Imperial Hohenzollern family crypt. Prince Friedrich Ludwig's sarcophagus is among 100 held here.*

VISITORS' CHECKLIST

Map H3. Am Lustgarten.
Tel 20 26 91 19. Open daily.
Adm charge. Guided tours.
Concerts. Evensong in English
6pm Thu. Church service Sun.
www.berlinerdom.de

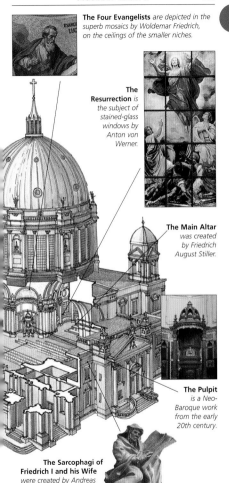

The Four Evangelists are depicted in the superb mosaics by Woldemar Friedrich, on the ceilings of the smaller niches.

The Resurrection is the subject of stained-glass windows by Anton von Werner.

The Main Altar was created by Friedrich August Stüler.

The Pulpit is a Neo-Baroque work from the early 20th century.

The Sarcophagi of Friedrich I and his Wife were created by Andreas Schlüter. The sculpture on Sophie Charlotte's sarcophagus depicts Death.

Pergamonmuseum ❽

Map H3. Bodestrasse 1–3 (entrance Am Kupfergraben). Open daily. Adm charge.

The Pergamonmuseum was built in 1912–30 to a design by Alfred Messels and Ludwig Hoffmann. Housing one of the most famous collections of antiquities in Europe, it owes its name to the superb Pergamon Altar which takes pride of place in the main hall. The museum is undergoing redevelopment.

Pergamon Altar, featuring Athena

It remains open during renovations, which are due for completion in 2025.

The three collections – the Museum of Antiquities (Greek and Roman), the Museum of Near Eastern Antiquities and the Museum of Islamic Art – are the result of intensive, large-scale archaeological excavations by German expeditions to the Near and Middle East at the end of the 19th and start of the 20th century.

The collection of Greek and Roman antiquities began in the 17th century and grew until it was opened to the public in 1830, initially in the Altes Museum, and from 1930 in the new, purpose-built Pergamonmuseum. The highlight of the collection is the huge Pergamon Altar from the acropolis of the ancient city of Pergamon in Asia Minor. Other Pergamon structures from the same period are also kept here, including part of the Athena temple, together with Greek sculptures and ceramic art.

The most impressive exhibits in the Museum of Near Eastern Antiquities come from a royal collection begun during the 1880s. They include architecture, sculpture and jewellery from Babylon, Iran and Assyria. Of note is the magnificent Ishtar Gate and the Processional Way from ancient Babylon. Also on display are items from Persia, Syria and Palestine, including a basalt bird from Tell Halaf.

Highlights of the Museum of Islamic Art include Wilhelm von Bode's collection of carpets, part of a Jordanian desert palace and a 13th-century *mibrab*, the niche in a mosque that shows the direction of Mecca. Also included are miniature paintings, everyday objects and an Ottoman reception room.

The Ishtar Gate, which dates from the 6th century BC

The Bodemuseum, designed to fit the wedged end of Museum Island

Bodemuseum ⑨

Map H3. Monbijoubrücke (Bodestrasse 1–3). Open daily. Adm charge.

This museum, built in 1897–1904, is named after the director of the Berlin state museums at the time. Its greatest attraction is the coin collection which includes some of the world's oldest pieces, from Athens in the 6th century BC. The museum also displays works by many notable sculptors including Tilman Riemenschneider, Gian Lorenzo Bernini, Donatello and Antonio Canova, among others.

Marstall ⑩

Map H4. Schlossplatz/Breite Strasse 36–8.

The huge complex of the Royal Stables contains a fragment of the old structure built in 1669, on the side of Breite Strasse, Berlin's only surviving early Baroque building. The other wings were built between 1898 and 1901 to designs by Ernst von Ihle, modelled on Baroque plans from 1700.

Ribbeckhaus ⑪

Map H4. Breite Strasse 35.

Four picturesque gables crown the only Renaissance building left in central Berlin, built c.1624 for Hans Georg von Ribbeck, a court counsellor. After he sold the house to Anna Sophie of Brunswick it became crown property, and when a storey was added, the gables were retained by royal decree. The house has a late Renaissance portal, replaced in 1960 with a copy. It displays the coat of arms of the first owners. Original features include the beautiful wrought-iron grilles on the ground-floor windows.

Ornate portal of the Ribbeckhaus

The Märkisches Museum, in the brick-Gothic style popular in the region

Märkisches Museum 🕑

Map J4. Am Köllnischen Park 5. Open Tue–Sun. Adm charge.

This architectural pastiche resembling a medieval monastery was built by Ludwig Hoffmann in 1901–8. It houses a collection relating to the history of Berlin and the Mark Brandenburg region, from the time of the earliest settlers to the present.

Boats moored along Märkisches Ufer, including a summer café

Märkisches Ufer 🕓

Map J4.

This picturesque Spree river promenade gives a good impression of the city as it once looked in the 18th and 19th centuries. Eight attractive houses have been carefully conserved. The two Neo-Baroque houses at Nos. 16 and 18 used to exhibit paintings by Otto Nagel. They now house the photographic archives for the state museums of Berlin.

Ermeler-Haus 🕔

Map J4. Märkisches Ufer 10.

With its Neo-Classical façade, this house is one of the most handsome villas in Berlin. It was once the town house of Wilhelm Ferdinand Ermeler, a wealthy tobacco merchant and shopkeeper. In 1825 it was remodelled to Ermeler's specifications, including a frieze alluding to aspects of the tobacco business. It was built on the opposite bank of the river, on Fischerinsel, but in 1968 it was dismantled and rebuilt on this site. Restorers have recreated much of the original façade. The Rococo furniture dates from c.1760 and the 18th-century staircase has been rebuilt.

The Neo-Classical Ermeler-Haus

Gertraudenbrücke ⑮

Map H4.

One of Berlin's more interesting bridges, this one connects Fischer Island with Spittelmarkt at the point where St Gertrude's Hospital once stood. The Gertraudenbrücke was designed by Otto Stahn and built in 1894. In the middle of the bridge is a bronze statue of the hospital's patron saint, St Gertrude, by Rudolf Siemering. A 13th-century Christian mystic, St Gertrude is shown here as a Benedictine abbess. Leaning over a poor youth she hands him a lily (symbol of virginity), a distaff (care for the poor) and a vessel filled with wine (love). The pedestal is surrounded by mice, a reference to the fact that Gertrude is patron saint of farmland and graves – both often frequented by mice.

St Gertrude as an abbess

Nicolai-Haus ⑯

Map H4. Brüderstrasse 13. Open Tue–Sun. Adm charge.

Built c.1710, the Nicolai-Haus is a fine example of Baroque architecture with a magnificent original oak staircase. The house has become famous as the home and bookshop of the publisher and controversial writer Christoph Friedrich Nicolai (1733–1811), who acquired the house around 1788. He had it rebuilt to a Neo-Classical design by Karl Friedrich Zelter. Regular visitors included the philosopher Moses Mendelssohn and literary notables Gotthold Ephraim Lessing, Johann Gottfried Schadow and Daniel Chodowiecki, all of whom are listed on a wall plaque. The rear wing features a fine staircase from the destroyed Weydinger-Haus.

STREET LIFE

RESTAURANTS AND CAFÉS

Brauhaus Georgbräu
Map H4. Spreeufer 4.
Tel 242 42 44. **Moderate**
Popular brewpub serving typical Berlin cuisine.

Historischer Hafen Berlin
Map J4. Märkisches Ufer 1z.
Tel 21 47 32 57.
Over 20 historical ships are

moored here. Deckshaus has a café-bistro, Renate Angelika a display on local waterways.

BARS AND PUBS

Factory Restaurant & Bar
Map J4. Hotel art'otel Berlin-Mitte. Wallstrasse 70–73.
Food and art in historic hall.

See p80 for price codes.

EAST OF THE CENTRE

This part of the Mitte district is the historic heart
of the city, where the twin towns of Cölln and
Berlin merged in the 13th century. Later, it was
a trade and residential district, but the Old Town
survived until World War II. The GDR replaced
the buildings to the north with a vast square and
built the television tower, Berlin's tallest structure.

SIGHTS AT A GLANCE

KEY

🚉	Railway station
Ⓤ	U-Bahn
Ⓢ	S-Bahn

0 metres	600
0 yards	600

◀ *One of the goddesses surrounding Neptune in the Neptunbrunnen*

Riverside buildings in the charming Nikolaiviertel

Rotes Rathaus ❶

Map J3. Rathausstrasse 15.
Open Mon–Fri.

The office of the mayor and
the political centre of power
in the city, the Red Town
Hall was built in 1861–9
by Hermann Friedrich
Waesemann. A continuous
frieze, the "stone chronicle",
was added in 1879. It features
scenes and figures from the
city's history, economy and
science. The town hall was
badly damaged in World War
II and rebuilt in 1951–8. It is
called "red" because of its red
brickwork, not its Socialist
past. Today it is also known
as the Berliner Rathaus,
reflecting its present status.

*Rotes Rathaus, built with red bricks
from Brandenburg province*

Nikolaiviertel and Nikolaikirche ❷

Map H/J4. Nikolaikirche: Nikolaikirchplatz. Open daily. Adm charge.

The small St Nicholas
Quarter on the bank of the
Spree is a favourite place for
strolling. Some of Berlin's
oldest houses stood here
until they were destroyed in
World War II. The GDR government rebuilt the entire
medieval town in 1979–87 –
a few remaining houses
were restored and other historic buildings were rebuilt
as replicas. Its mews and
alleys are now home to
small shops, bars and cafés.

Nikolaikirche was the
oldest sacred building in
historic Berlin, started c.1230
and completed in stages
by the mid-15th century.
A magnificent Gothic brick
hall-church, it featured a
chancel with an ambulatory
and a row of low chapels.
In 1877 Hermann Blanken-
stein removed most of its
Baroque modifications and
rebuilt the front towers.

Destroyed by bombing in 1945 and rebuilt in 1980–87, the church has undergone a massive renovation. It now hosts an exhibition on Berlin's history, as well as its famous organ concerts. The tower is also open to visitors.

Ephraim-Palais

Map H4. Poststrasse 16. Open Tue–Sun. Adm charge.

This Baroque palace was built by Friedrich Wilhelm Diterichs in 1766 for Nathan Veitel Heinrich Ephraim, Frederick the Great's mint master and court jeweller. During the widening of the Mühlendamm bridge in 1935 the palace was demolished, possibly in part because of the owner's Jewish origins. Part of the façade was stored and in 1983 this was sent to East Berlin and used in the reconstruction of the palace, which was erected a few metres from its original site. One of the first-floor rooms features a restored Baroque ceiling by Andreas Schlüter, originally in Palais Wartenberg and dismantled in 1889. Ephraim-Palais currently houses a branch of the Berlin City Museum.

Neptunbrunnen

Neptunbrunnen ❹

Map H3. Spandauer Strasse (Rathausvorplatz).

This splendid Neo-Baroque fountain is a delight on the main axis of the town hall building. Created in 1891 by Reinhold Begas to stand in front of the southern wall of the former Stadtschloss (Berlin Castle), it was moved here in 1969. Neptune, at the centre of the fountain, is surrounded by four figures representing Germany's greatest rivers of the time: the Rhine, the Vistula, the Oder and the Elbe. The naturalism of the composition and the attention to detail, such as the beautiful bronze fish, crayfish, snails and fishing nets, are noteworthy.

Ephraim-Palais, at the junction of Poststrasse and Mühlendamm

Marienkirche ❻

Work on St Mary's Church started in
1270. In 1790, the 15th-century tower
was crowned with a dome by Langhans.
The early-Gothic hall design and lavish
decorative touches make this one of
Berlin's most interesting churches. In
2008 a glass atrium was built
inside the church tower.

The Tower *is
crowned by a dome
featuring both
Baroque and
Neo-Gothic
elements.*

Crucifixion (1562),
*by Michael Rihestein,
painted in the
Mannerist style,
depicts Christ
flanked by Moses
and St John
the Baptist.*

The Retable, *located by
the main altar, dates from
1510 and features the
figures of three monks.*

VISITORS' CHECKLIST

Map H3. Karl-Liebknecht-
Strasse 8. Tel 242 44 67.
Open daily. Adm free. Guided
tours available. Organ recitals.
Church service Sun.
www.marienkirche-berlin.de

Main entrance

The Pulpit *is one of Andreas Schlüter's masterpieces, carved from alabaster and completed in 1703. Standing by the fourth pillar, it is decorated with bas-reliefs of St John the Baptist and the Virtues.*

The von Röbel Family Tomb *was probably built after 1630, by Anton von Werner.*

The Main Altar *was designed by Andreas Krüger in the Baroque style c.1762.*

The Baptismal Font, *dating from 1437, is supported by three Gothic dragons and decorated with the figures of Jesus, Mary and the Apostles.*

Heiliggeistkapelle ⑤

Map H3. Spandauer Strasse 1. Free.

The Chapel of the Holy Spirit, built in the second half of the 13th century and rebuilt in the 15th century, is a fine example of Gothic brick construction and the only surviving hospital chapel in Berlin. The east façade is particularly noteworthy. The hospital itself was demolished in 1825.

Marienkirche ⑥

See pp30–31.

The Fernsehturm

Fernsehturm ⑦

Map J3. Panoramastrasse 1a. Open daily. Adm charge.

The television tower remains to this day the city's tallest structure, and one of the tallest in Europe. At 368 m (1,207 ft), it affords great views of up to 40 km (25 miles) in good weather. The tower was built in 1969 to a design by a team of architects including Fritz Dieter and Günter Franke, with the help of Swedish engineering experts. However, the idea for such a colossal, Socialist-Realist tower in Berlin came much earlier, from Hermann Henselmann (creator of the nearby Karl-Marx-Allee development).

In the steel-clad sphere, the viewing platform is 203 m (666 ft) above the ground. The Sphere Restaurant above, the main attraction, rotates around its axis once every 30 minutes, giving unrivalled views over all of Berlin in good weather. Unfortunately, the tower is served by small lifts and there can be long queues at peak times.

Alexanderplatz ⑧

Map J3.

This square was once the site of a cattle and wool market. It was later renamed after Tsar Alexander I, who visited Berlin in 1805. In time, "Alex" became one of the town's busiest spots. Damaged in World War II, the square was then surrounded by characterless edifices for many years. It has now been redeveloped into a bustling metropolitan hub with several large shopping malls, including Galeria Kaufhof and Alexa.

World time clock on "Alex"

Stadtgericht

Map J3. Littenstrasse 11–17.
Open Mon–Fri. Free.

The huge Neo-Baroque Courts of Justice were built in 1896–1905 to designs by Thomer and Mönnich and finished by Schmalz. The building was partly demolished in 1969 but it is still worth seeing, because it hides an Art Nouveau gem – the magnificent staircase. The slim Neo-Gothic pillars and the balustrades further enhance the interior.

Gaststätte Zur letzten Instanz

Gaststätte Zur letzten Instanz ⑩

Map J4. Waisenstrasse 14–16.

One of the oldest inns in Berlin, the Inn of the Last Instance is one of four picturesque houses on Waisenstrasse built in medieval times. Their present form dates from the 18th century, and they were rebuilt after World War II. The Inn, first established in 1621, was frequently patronized by lawyers. It is still popular today.

The fairytale Stadtgericht staircase

STREET LIFE

RESTAURANTS

Mutter Hoppe
Map H4. Rathausstrasse 21.
Tel 247 20 603. **Moderate**
Cosy restaurant serving hearty Berlin cuisine.

Reinhard's
Map H4. Poststrasse 28.
Tel 242 52 95. **Expensive**
Charming, Roaring Twenties setting, international cuisine, steak a speciality.

Zum Paddenwirt
Map J4. Nikolaikirchplatz 6.
Tel 242 63 82. **Moderate**
Traditional Berlin fare.

BARS AND PUBS

Historische Weinstuben
Map H4. Poststrasse 23.
Popular wine bar with a good range of wines. Serves food.

Zum Nussbaum
Map H4. Am Nussbaum 3.
Draught beers and Berlin fare in a 16th-century-style inn in the Nikolaiviertel.

Zur letzten Instanz
Map J4. Waisenstrasse 16.
German beer and food in Berlin's oldest inn.

SHOPPING

Alexa
Map J3. Grunerstrasse 20.
Berlin's largest centrally located mall, just off Alexanderplatz.

Galeria Kaufhof
Map J3. Alexanderplatz 9.
Largest department store in East Berlin, stocks everything.

See p80 for price codes.

NORTH OF THE CENTRE

The area northwest of Alexanderplatz is the former Spandauer Vorstadt. The Scheunenviertel (Barn Quarter), in its eastern half, was the centre of Berlin's Jewish community in the 19th century. In the 1920s it attracted artists, writers and political activists. This part of Berlin has become fashionable again, and its alleys and courtyards are popular with tourists and Berliners alike.

SIGHTS AT A GLANCE

Streets and Parks
Alte and Neue
  Schönhauser Strasse **10**
Monbijoupark **4**
Oranienburger Strasse **3**
Sophienstrasse **9**

Churches and Synagogues
Neue Synagoge **1**
Sophienkirche **8**

Museums
Brecht-Weigel-
  Gedenkstätte **15**
Centrum Judaicum **2**
Hamburger Bahnhof **17**
Museum für Naturkunde **16**

Theatres
Berliner Ensemble **14**
Friedrichstadtpalast **12**
Volksbühne **11**

Cemeteries
Alter Jüdischer Friedhof **7**
Dorotheenstädtischer
  Friedhof **13**

Others
Gedenkstätte Berliner
  Mauer **18**
Gedenkstätte Grosse
  Hamburger Strasse **6**
Hackesche Höfe **5**

SEE ALSO

• Street Life p41.

KEY

🚌 Bus terminus
🚉 Railway station
🚃 Tram stop
Ⓤ U-Bahn
Ⓢ S-Bahn

| 0 metres | 800 |
| 0 yards | 800 |

◄ The first courtyard in Hackesche Höfe

Neue Synagoge ❶

Map H3. Oranienburger Strasse 28–30. Open Sun–Fri. Services Fri pm, Sat am, holidays. Adm charge.

The New Synagogue, built by Eduard Knoblauch in 1859–66, was once the largest in Europe. Its advanced design – including space for 3,000 worshippers, and the use of iron in the roof and galleries – put it at the forefront of 19th-century civil engineering. In 1938, it survived *Kristallnacht* (the looting and burning of Jewish property by the Nazis). However, after World War II damage, it was demolished in 1958. It was rebuilt in 1988–95.

Centrum Judaicum ❷

Map H3. Oranienburger Strasse 28–30. Open Sun–Fri. Adm charge.

The Centre occupies the former premises of the Jewish community council. It houses a library, archives and a research centre on the history and culture of Berlin's Jews. All visitors to the Jewish Centre must undergo a strict security check.

Neue Synagoge's gilded dome

Oranienburger Strasse ❸

Map H3/4.

Oranienburger Strasse is home to many of Berlin's most popular nightspots. People of all ages flock here to visit the area's numerous cafés, restaurants and bars. The district has traditionally been a centre for alternative culture. It is home to the famous former Tacheles centre for the arts as well as many good art galleries that remain in this area. As you stroll around the district it is worth looking out for a number of interesting buildings, such as the Postfuhramt or the house at Oranienburger Strasse No. 71–2, built by Christian Friedrich Becherer in 1789 for the Great National Masonic Lodge of Germany.

Façade of the former Tacheles arts centre on Oranienburger Strasse

A courtyard in the Hackesche Höfe

Monbijoupark **4**

Map H3. Oranienburger Strasse.

This small park between Oranienburger Strasse and the Spree river was once the grounds of the Monbijou Palace. Damaged by bombing during World War II, the ruined palace was finally dismantled in 1960. The well-kept park features a marble bust of the poet Adelbert von Chamisso, and there is also a paddling pool for children.

Hackesche Höfe **5**

Map H3. Rosenthaler Strasse 40–41.

Berlin's largest and most attractive group of restored commercial buildings, Hackesche Höfe extends between Oranienburger and Rosenthaler Strasse and up to Sophienstrasse in the east.

The early 20th-century complex, comprising nine linked courtyards, was designed by Kurt Berndt and August Endell, two leading exponents of Art Nouveau. In the first courtyard, glazed tiles are laid out in vibrantly coloured geometric patterns, covering the whole building. Today, the many shops, restaurants, cafés and art galleries in the complex are busy day and night.

Gedenkstätte Grosse Hamburger Strasse **6**

Map H3. Grosse Hamburger Strasse.

Before 1939, this street in Berlin's Jewish quarter was home to several Jewish schools, an old people's home and the city's oldest Jewish cemetery. During World War II the home was used as a detention centre for thousands of Berlin Jews condemned to death in the camps at Auschwitz and Theresienstadt. The building was later destroyed, and in its place now stands a monument representing a group of Jews being led to their deaths. Nearby is a modest commemorative plaque.

The Grosse Hamburger Strasse Memorial to concentration camp victims

Alter Jüdischer Friedhof **7**

Map H3. Grosse Hamburger Strasse. Free.

The Old Jewish Cemetery, established in 1672, provided a resting place for over 12,000 Berliners, including the philosopher Moses Mendelssohn. In 1827 it was declared full. After this date, Jews were buried in cemeteries in Schönhauser Allee and in Herbert-Baum-Strasse. The Old Cemetery was destroyed by the Nazis in 1943, and in 1945 the site became a park.

Inside Sophienkirche, showing the original 18th-century pulpit

Sophienkirche **8**

Map H3. Grosse Hamburger Strasse 29–31. Open Wed & Sat. Sun service 10am. Free.

This small Baroque church was founded in 1712 by Queen Sophie Luisa. The tower, built in 1729–35, is by Johann Friedrich Grael. It contains 18th-century furnishings, including the pulpit and the font. The small cemetery has some 18th-century gravestones.

Sophienstrasse: 18th-century houses restored in the 1980s

Sophienstrasse **9**

Map H3.

This narrow street has been beautifully restored and now looks much as it did in the late 18th century. A number of interesting galleries, bars, boutiques and workshops are now based here.

Alte and Neue Schönhauser Strasse **10**

Map H3.

Alte Schönhauser Strasse is one of the oldest streets in Spandauer Vorstadt. In past times this lively road was full of small private shops and factories and it is now a mix of traditional and trendy shops, restaurants and bars.

Alte Schönhauser Strasse

Volksbühne ⓫

Map J3. Rosa-Luxemburg-Platz.

Founded in the early 1900s, this theatre owes its existence to the efforts of the 100,000 members of the Freie Volksbühne (Free People's Theatre Society). The original theatre was built to a design by Oskar Kaufmann in 1913. During the 1920s it became famous under the directorship of Erwin Piscator (1893–1966). Destroyed during World War II, the theatre was rebuilt in the early 1950s to a new design by Hans Richter.

Friedrichstadtpalast ⓬

Map G3. Friedrichstrasse 107.

The original palais, dating back to the late 1800s, was much loved for its revues, variety shows and TV spectaculars. It suffered bomb damage and was replaced with this gigantic, Oriental-style theatre complex in the 1980s. Nearly 2,000 seats are arranged around a large podium, used as a circus arena, a swimming pool and an ice-rink. There is also a huge hi-tech stage and a small cabaret theatre.

The eye-catching façade of the Friedrichstadtpalast

Dorotheenstädtischer Friedhof ⓭

Map G2. Chausseestrasse 126. Open daily.

A tranquil, tree-filled oasis, this small cemetery, established in 1763, is the final resting place of many German luminaries, including Heinrich Mann, Bertolt Brecht and Georg Wilhelm Hegel. It was enlarged between 1814 and 1826, but in 1899, after the extension of Hannoversche Strasse, the southern section of the cemetery was sold and its graves moved. Many of the monuments are outstanding works of art, coming from the workshops of some of the most prominent Berlin architects, including Karl Friedrich Schinkel and Johann Gottfried Schadow, who are also buried here.

The Brecht family graves in Dorotheenstädtischer Friedhof

Bertolt Brecht monument in front of the Berliner Ensemble

Berliner Ensemble ⑭

Map G3. Bertolt-Brecht-Platz 1.

Built in 1891–2 as a Neo-Baroque structure, the theatre soon became famous for staging important premières, including Hauptmann's *The Weavers* (1895) and Brecht's *Threepenny Opera* (1928). After its destruction in World War II, it was rebuilt with a simpler exterior and returned to prominence with the Berliner Ensemble directed by Brecht and his wife.

Brecht-Weigel-Gedenkstätte ⑮

Map G2. Chausseestrasse 125. Open Tue, Wed, Fri & Sat am; all day Thu & Sun. Adm charge.

After exile in the USA, Bertolt Brecht, one of the 20th century's greatest playwrights, returned to East Berlin in 1948 and lived here with his wife, Helene Weigel, in 1953–6. On display are original furnishings, photographs and papers. The second floor has an archive of his work.

Museum für Naturkunde ⑯

Map G2. Invalidenstrasse 43. Open Tue–Sun. Adm charge.

One of the largest natural history museums in the world, this collection contains over 60 million exhibits. Highlights include the world's largest original dinosaur skeleton and extensive collections of shells, butterflies, stuffed birds and mammals, as well as a large quantity of minerals and meteorites. A favourite with young children is Knut the polar bear, a star draw of Berlin Zoo in 2007–11.

Hamburger Bahnhof: modern art in a former railway station

Hamburger Bahnhof ⑰

Map F2. Invalidenstrasse 50–51. Open Tue–Sun. Adm charge.

This museum is situated in a specially adapted Neo-Renaissance building that was formerly the Hamburg Railway station, dating from 1847. It holds modern paintings, installations and multimedia art. Following extensive refurbishment by Josef Paul Kleihues, it was opened to the public in 1996. The neon installation surrounding the façade is the work of Dan Flavin. The museum has works from the Erich Marx collection, including some by Andy Warhol, Roy

Berliners dismantle the Berlin Wall in 1989

Lichtenstein and Joseph Beuys. It also has contemporary art donated by the Neue Nationalgalerie and a continually changing selection from the world-renowned Flick Collection of art from the second half of the 20th century, including works by Marcel Duchamp, Mike Kelly, Bruce Nauman and Luc Tuymans.

The result is one of the best modern art museums in Europe, featuring film, video, music and design as well as the more traditional painting and sculpture.

Gedenkstätte Berliner Mauer ⑱

Map G2. Bernauer Strasse 111. Open Tue–Sun. Free.

In August 1961, the East German authorities closed the border to West Berlin and encircled the western part of the city with a 4-m (13-ft) double wall, patrolled by guards with dogs. The wall was breached in 1989 and later dismantled. This memorial contains the last remaining stretch of the Berlin Wall, with preserved grounds behind it.

STREET LIFE

RESTAURANTS AND CAFÉS

Barcomi's Deli
Map H3. Sophienstrasse 21. Tel 28 59 83 63. **Moderate**
This café serves great cakes and roasts its own coffee.

Brecht-Keller
Map G2. Chausseestrasse 125. Tel 282 38 43. **Moderate**
Bertolt Brecht once lived here. Hearty food is prepared to Helene Weigel's recipes.

Hackescher Hof
Map H3. Rosenthaler Strasse 40. Tel 283 52 93. **Expensive**
The best restaurant in Hackesche Höfe, offering mainly regional fare.

BARS AND CLUBS

CCCP Club
Map H3. Rosenthaler Strasse 71.
Russian disco and burlesque.

Meilenstein
Map H3. Oranienburger Strasse 7.
Traditional Berlin pub.

See p80 for price codes.

TIERGARTEN

This part of the city boasts a vast park and many of Berlin's finest museums and historic buildings, including the restored Reichstag. The Potsdamer Platz, once again a lively neighbourhood, has become an exciting showcase of modern architecture.

SIGHTS AT A GLANCE

Museums and Galleries

Bauhaus-Archiv ⑩
Bendlerblock ⑥
Gemäldegalerie ⑧
Kunstbibliothek ④
Kunstgewerbemuseum ⑦
Kupferstichkabinett ③
Musikinstrumenten-
  Museum ①
Neue Nationalgalerie ⑤

Districts, Squares and Parks

Diplomatenviertel ⑪
Hansaviertel ⑮
Potsdamer Platz ⑭
Regierungsviertel ⑱
Tiergarten ⑫

Historic Buildings

Haus der Kulturen
  der Welt ⑰
Philharmonie and
  Kammermusiksaal ②
Reichstag ⑲
Schloss Bellevue ⑯
Siegessäule ⑬
Sowjetisches Ehrenmal ⑳
Villa von der Heydt ⑨

SEE ALSO

• *Street Life p53.*

KEY

🚌 Bus terminus

Ⓤ U-Bahn

Ⓢ S-Bahn

| 0 metres | 800 |
| 0 yards | 800 |

◄ *The Haus der Kulturen der Welt, a great 1950s edifice*

Musikinstrumenten-Museum ❶

Map F4. Tiergartenstrasse 1 (entrance Ben-Gurion-Strasse). Open Tue–Sun. Adm charge.

Behind the Philharmonie, the little Museum of Musical Instruments houses over 800 exhibits in a collection dating from 1888. Fascinating displays show each instrument's development from the 16th century to the present day. Exhibits include a Jean Marius harpsichord and Stradivarius violins. Most spectacular of all is the 1929 Wurlitzer cinema organ (tours and concerts at 6pm Thursdays and noon on Saturdays).

Philharmonie and Kammermusiksaal ❷

Map F4. Herbert-von-Karajan-Strasse 1. Open daily. Adm charge for tour (1pm).

The Philharmonie, designed by Hans Scharoun in 1960–63, was the first new structure in the Kulturforum. Boasting superb acoustics, it is home to the Berlin Philharmonic Orchestra. After Herbert von Karajan and Claudio Abbado, Sir Simon Rattle became the conductor in 2002. The Kammermusiksaal, by Wisniewski after sketches by Scharoun, was added in 1984–7.

Portrait of Dürer's mother, kept in the Kupferstichkabinett

Kupferstichkabinett ❸

Map F4. Matthäikirchplatz 8. Open Tue–Sun. Adm charge.

The print collections of East and West Berlin were united in 1994 in this building. Despite wartime losses the gallery can boast around 2,000 engraver's plates, over 520,000 prints and 80,000 drawings and watercolours. Unfortunately, only a few can be exposed to daylight, so the museum mounts only temporary displays of selected works. However, stored items can be viewed by arrangement. The collection holds work from every major artist from the Middle Ages to the present, including pieces by Botticelli, Dürer, Rembrandt and the Dutch Masters, Watteau, Goya, Daumier and painters of the Brücke art movement.

The tent-like Philharmonie and Kammermusiksaal

The Bendlerblock, now home to the Federal Ministry of Defence

Kunstbibliothek

Map F4. Matthäikirchplatz 6. Open Tue–Sun. Adm charge.

The Art Library not only has a wide range of publications about the arts, it also houses a huge collection of posters, adverts and other forms of design. Worth seeing is a display on the history of fashion and a vast collection of architectural items. These include 30,000 original plans and drawings by architects such as Johann Balthasar Neumann, Paul Wallot and Erich Mendelssohn.

Neue Nationalgalerie

Map F5. Potsdamer Strasse 50. Closed until 2017.

Based in a building by Mies van der Rohe, the gallery exhibits mainly 20th-century German art, with temporary exhibitions of contemporary art. Also represented are artists of the late 19th century, such as Edvard Munch, Ferdinand Hodler and Oskar Kokoschka.

Bendlerblock (Gedenkstätte Deutscher Widerstand)

Map F5. Stauffenbergstrasse 13–14. Open daily. Free.

This collection of buildings was erected during the Third Reich. During World War II the Bendlerblock housed the headquarters of the Wehrmacht (German army). It was here that a group of officers planned the assassination of Hitler on 20 July 1944. When the attempt failed, the conspirators were quickly arrested. General Ludwig Beck was ordered to commit suicide (he did not succeed), while the others were shot in the Bendlerblock courtyard. A monument commemorating this event, designed by Richard Scheibe in 1953, stands where the executions were carried out. On the building's upper floor, an exhibition of over 5,000 images and documents tells the story of the German anti-Nazi resistance movements.

Kunstgewerbemuseum 🄼

Map F4. Matthäikirchplatz 4–6.
Open Tue–Sun. Adm charge.

The Museum of Decorative
Arts holds superb examples
of craft and decorative art.
A new gallery shows 18th–
20th-century costumes and
fashion accessories.

Middle Ages

Much of this collection is
devoted to sacred art from
church treasuries. Exhibits
include medieval goldwork
from the church treasuries
of Enger, and the Guelph
treasury from Brunswick.

Renaissance

Italian majolica, 15th- and
16th-century Venetian glass,
porcelain from Limoges and
richly decorated tableware
from the civic treasury at
Lüneburg are among the
Renaissance pieces.

Baroque

Star exhib-
its include
German and
Bohemian
glass and
18th-cen-
tury ceramic
pieces.

*A book cover (1339) with silver,
gems and pearls*

The porcelain section has
Böttger ceramics, Meissen
porcelain and items from
Berlin's Königliche
Porzellan-Manufaktur
(Royal Porcelain Factory).

Neo-Classical and
Art Nouveau

The Neo-Classical period is
represented by porcelain
from famous European and
Russian factories, French and
German silver, glassware
and furniture. Stunning
Art Nouveau works on
display include glass
vases by Gallé,
and jewellery
and glassware
by Tiffany
and Lalique.

20th Century

Art Deco is well
represented; items
include a Gertrud
Kant tea service
and an ebony-
decorated silver
coffee set by
Jean Puiforcat.
The gallery owns
a wide range of
ceramics, furniture and
items of everyday use.

*Meissen porcelain figures (1741)
designed by J J Kändler*

Titian's Venus with the Organ Player *(1550–52)*

Gemäldegalerie ❽

Map F4. Matthäikirchplatz 4–6.
Open Tue–Sun. Adm charge.

The Art Gallery holds
a superb collection of paintings, with exhibits from all
the major European schools.

German Painting
The collection of earlier
German art comprises
religious paintings and altar-
pieces from the 13th to 16th
centuries and features work
by Albrecht Dürer and
a portrait by Holbein the
Younger. Paintings from the
17th and 18th centuries are
displayed separately.

Dutch and Flemish Painting
Highlights among the Dutch
exhibits are van der Goes'
The Adoration of the Magi
and works by Hieronymus
Bosch, Vermeer and Rem-
brandt. The Flemish section
has pieces by Rubens, van
Dyck and Brueghel the Elder.

Italian Painting
The gallery's large collection
of Italian art features works
by 14th-century masters

such as Giotto, 15th-century
paintings by Fra Angelico,
Masaccio and Botticelli and
later works by Raphael, as
well as great paintings from
the Venetian school.

French, English and Spanish Painting
French paintings range from
early 15th-century works
and pieces by Fouquet and
Poussin to 18th-century gems
by Boucher and Watteau.
A Velázquez portrait is the
pride of the Spanish section,
while English art includes
portraits by Joshua Reynolds
and Thomas Gainsborough.

Portrait of Hieronymus Holzschuher
(1529) by Albrecht Dürer

Villa von der Heydt ❾

Map E5. Von-der-Heydt-Strasse 18.

Restored in 1967, this late Neo-Classical villa is one of the few surviving examples of the architectural villa style typical of the old Tiergarten. Its neat gardens are adorned with busts by Reinhold Begas. It was built in 1860–62, to plans by Hermann Ende and G A Linke, for one of Berlin's most elegant residential areas at the time. Since 1980, the Prussian Heritage Foundation has had its headquarters here.

The elegant Villa von der Heydt

Bauhaus-Archiv ❿

Map E5. Klingelhöferstrasse 14. Open Wed–Mon. Adm charge.

The Bauhaus school of art, started by Walter Gropius in 1919, was one of the most influential of the 20th century. The white building with its glass-panelled gables was adapted by Alexander Cvijanovic from Walter Gropius' plans and built in 1976–9. It houses the archive, library and exhibition halls for temporary displays.

The gleaming Bauhaus-Archiv

Diplomatenviertel ⓫

Map E4.

Although consulates existed in the Tiergarten area from 1918, the establishment of a diplomatic district along the southern edge of the Tiergarten did not take place until Hitler's Third Reich. During 1938–43, large embassies representing the Axis Powers, Italy and Japan, were built here, but many of the buildings did not survive World War II bombing.

Tiergartenstrasse is now the home to new diplomatic buildings. The Austrian embassy, by Hans Hollein, stands at the junction of Stauffenbergstrasse, next to the embassies of Egypt and India. At Nos. 21–3 the pre-World War II Italian embassy still stands, next to a copy of the first Japanese embassy. Between Klingelhöferstrasse and Rauchstrasse stand five supermodern, interlinked embassies, representing Norway, Sweden, Denmark, Finland and Iceland.

The Austrian embassy

The Lortzing Memorial, one of 70 statues in the Tiergarten

Tiergarten ⑫

Map F4.

The largest park in Berlin, situated at the centre of the city, occupies more than 200 ha (495 acres). Once the Elector's hunting reserve, it was transformed into a park by Peter Joseph Lenné in the 1830s. Damage during and after World War II included the destruc- tion of the Triumphal Avenue. Replanting has now reinstated the Tiergarten as a favourite recreation area. Its avenues are lined with statues of figures such as Goethe and Wagner. At the centre is a huge roundabout called Grosser Stern (Great Star), surrounded by monuments, such as that of Bismarck, the German Chancellor (1815–98).

Victory, known as the "Goldelse"

Siegessäule ⑬

Map E4. Grosser Stern. Open daily. Adm charge.

The triumphal column, based on a design by Johann Heinrich Strack, was built to commemorate victory in the Prussian-Danish war of 1864. After further victories against Austria (1866) and France (1871), the gilded figure of Victory by Friedrich Drake was added to the top. The monument originally stood in front of the Reichstag, but was moved to its present location in 1938. The base is decorated with bas-reliefs depicting battles, while higher up a mosaic frieze by Anton von Werner shows the founding of the German Empire in 1871. An observation terrace at the top of the column offers mag- nificent vistas over Berlin.

Potsdamer Platz ⓮

Map G4.

Berlin's post-Wall architectural revitalization is exemplified by Potsdamer Platz, which has been transformed into a busy, if slightly sterile, business and leisure hub. In the Roaring Twenties, Potsdamer Platz was Europe's busiest plaza. Developed from a green park in 1831 and named after a city gate (Potsdamer Tor), the square eventually included a railway station and an underground train line, plus 31 tram and bus lines. At the turn of the 20th century, it became the centre of Berlin's nightlife and hosted the first radio transmission in Germany (1923). The square was almost destroyed by Allied bombardments during the final Battle of Berlin in April 1945. It became a vast open space in the shadow of the Berlin Wall where tourists, standing on high observation platforms, could peek over.

New development

The redevelopment of Potsdamer Platz started in 1992, after Germany's reunification. Major multinationals, such as Daimler AG and Sony, invested a total of $25 billion, creating Europe's largest construction site.

Today, Berlin's old hub is again a dynamic centre and a jewel of modern architecture, with trailblazing design by Renzo Piano, Helmut Jahn, Arata Isozaki and others. The square boasts cinemas, restaurants and shops, and a large Christmas market throughout December.

Beisheim Center

Lenné-, Bellevue- and Ebertstrasse.
This glass and steel building was designed by Berlin architects Hilmer, Sattler & Albrecht, with parts by David Chipperfield, for Otto Beisheim, a German entrepreneur. The centre houses several de luxe apartments, a luxurious Ritz-Carlton hotel, an elegant Marriott hotel and exclusive shops.

Façade of the Filmmuseum Berlin

Filmmuseum Berlin

Potsdamer Strasse 2 (Sony Center).
Open Tue–Sun. Adm charge.
The museum chronicles cinema from the first silent movies to modern science-fiction productions, focusing on German films from the successful 1920s. Other notable exhibits include films from the era of the Third Reich and the fascinating Marlene Dietrich collection.

Potsdamer Platz Arkaden

Alte Potsdamer Strasse 7. Open Mon–Sat.
The arcades house some 130 shops and restaurants on three floors, offering dishes from around the world.

Arkaden, popular with shoppers

Daimler AG's headquarters

Theater am Potsdamer Platz
Marlene-Dietrich-Platz 1. Open daily.

Berlin's largest musical stage is housed in this theatre, designed by Renzo Piano as part of the Quartier Potsdamer Platz. The basement houses the Adagio nightclub and also the popular casino, Spielbank Berlin. Jeff Koons' Balloon Flower sculpture adorns the square in front of the building. The complex is also the main forum for the Berlinale, Berlin's world-renowned film festival.

Interior of the cupola of the Sony Center, designed by Helmut Jahn

Sony Center
Potsdamer Strasse 2. Open daily.

This Helmut Jahn steel and glass building covers 4,013 sq m (43,195 sq ft). Under a high tent-like roof, the central piazza is surrounded by Sony's Europe headquarters, flats, restaurants and a mix of shops. The CineStar, a cinema with eight screens, the Filmmuseum Berlin and the Legoland Discovery Center are also here.

Quartier Potsdamerplatz
Around Alte Potsdamer Strasse. Viewing platform open daily. Adm charge.

This vast complex, built in 1993–8, comprises 19 modern buildings in different styles by Renzo Piano and Christoph Kohlbecker, leading down to the Landwehr Canal. On either side of Alte Potsdamer Strasse, the area's entrance is marked by two red-brick Werner Kollhoff skyscrapers.

Leipziger Platz
Map G4.

Leipziger Platz, just east of Potsdamer Platz, has been rebuilt. The octagonal square was created in 1732–4 and Schinkel and Lenné landscaped the area in the 19th century. No remains survived World War II, but buildings added later include a Dalí museum and a huge shopping mall.

Haus Huth
Alte Potsdamer Strasse 5. Open daily.

Designed by Conrad Heidenreich and Paul Michel in 1912, this building today houses Daimler's contemporary arts gallery, along with a restaurant, a café and a wine shop.

Rauschenberg's sculpture Riding Bikes, with Haus Huth behind

Hansaviertel

Map D/E3.

This area houses some of the best modern architecture in Berlin, built for the 1957 Internationale Bauausstellung (International Architectural Exhibition). An international team of architects, including Walter Gropius (Händelallee Nos. 3–9), Alvar Aalto (Klopstockstr. Nos. 30–32) and Oscar Niemeyer (Altonaer Str. Nos. 4–14), created a residential development on a former bombsite, surrounded by lush greenery.

Schloss Bellevue

Map H3. Spreeweg 1. Closed to the public.

This palace with its white Neo-Classical façade is now the official residence of the German Federal President. Built in 1786 by Philipp Daniel Boumann for the Prussian Prince August Ferdinand, it served as a royal residence until 1861. In 1935 it was refurbished to house a Museum of German Ethnology. In 1938, it was again remodelled as a hotel for guests of the Nazi government. After war damage, the palace was carefully restored, with the oval ballroom rebuilt to a design by Langhans. The palace is set in a park laid out to the original late 18th-century design.

The House of World Culture, known as "the pregnant oyster"

Haus der Kulturen der Welt

Map F3. John-Foster-Dulles-Allee 10. Open Tue–Sun.

Built in 1956–7 by Hugh Stubbins, this building was the intended American entry in the architecture competition "Interbau 1957". It became a symbol of freedom and modernity in West Berlin during the Cold War. After its partial collapse and reconstruction, it reopened in 1989 and is now used for world culture events.

Regierungsviertel

Map F3.

Axel Schultes and Charlotte Frank developed the bold concept for a new government district and integrated transport system, built in 1997–2003. While many of the buildings were designed by other architects, Schultes and Frank conceived the Bundeskanzleramt, the official residence of the German Chancellor, located opposite the Reichstag.

The dazzling white Neo-Classical façade of Schloss Bellevue

The Reichstag's main entrance

Reichstag ⑲

Map F3. Platz der Republik.
Dome open daily. Free.

One of the most symbolic buildings in Berlin, the Reichstag was erected in 1884–94 by Paul Wallot as a proud symbol of the German Reich. It was damaged by arson in 1933, an event the Nazis used as a pretext to arrest communists. The Reichstag was further damaged when the Russians entered Berlin at the end of World War II. In 1994–9,

British architect Sir Norman Foster turned the building into one of the most modern parliamentary buildings in the world. A modern meeting hall is crowned by a glass dome with a viewing gallery to signify open government.

Sowjetisches Ehrenmal ⑳

Map F4. Strasse des 17 Juni.

This huge monument was unveiled on 7 November 1945, the anniversary of the start of the Russian Revolution. Flanked by the first two tanks to enter the city, the monument commemorates over 300,000 Soviet soldiers who perished in the battle for Berlin at the end of World War II. The vast marble column was by Nicolai Sergiejev, while the figure on top, a soldier cast in bronze, is by Lev Kerbel. The monument is also a cemetery for some 5,000 Soviet casualties.

Soviet memorial

STREET LIFE

RESTAURANTS

Facil
Map F4. Potsdamer Strasse 3.
Tel 590 051 234. **Expensive**
Michelin-starred dishes.

Käfer im Bundestag
Map F3. Reichstag, Platz der Republik. Tel 226 29 90.
Moderate
Dine on the Reichstag's roof.

Vox
Map G4. Marlene-Dietrich-Platz 2. Tel 25 53 17 72. **Expensive**
One of Berlin's finest

restaurants, serving sushi and Mediterranean dishes.

BARS AND PUBS

Café am Neuen See
Map D4. Lichtensteinallee 1.
Berlin's most popular beer garden also serves pub food.

SHOPPING

Potsdamer Platz Arkaden
Map G4. Alte Potsdamer Strasse.
Popular shopping centre in spectacular modern building.

See p80 for price codes.

KREUZBERG

Late 19th-century Kreuzberg was a working-class district. After World War II, it became the home of artists, students and immigrants. Today it is an area of contrasts where luxury flats have sprung up next to dilapidated buildings. Some parts are Turkish; others house affluent young professionals. Above all, it is a vibrant place, with bazaars, clubs, restaurants, cinemas, theatres and galleries.

SIGHTS AT A GLANCE

Museums
Berlinische Galerie **5**
Checkpoint Charlie **4**
Deutsches
   Technikmuseum **6**
Jüdisches Museum **1**
Martin-Gropius-Bau **2**
Topographie des Terrors **3**

Historic Buildings
Riehmers Hofgarten **8**

Squares, Parks and Cemeteries
Friedhöfe vor dem
   Halleschen Tor **7**
Viktoriapark **9**

SEE ALSO

• *Street Life p59.*

KEY

🚌 Bus terminus

Ⓤ U-Bahn

Ⓢ S-Bahn

| 0 metres | 800 |
| 0 yards | 800 |

◀ *The magnificent waterfall in Viktoriapark, Kreuzberg*

Jüdisches Museum Berlin ❶

Map H5. Lindenstrasse 9–14.
Open daily. Adm charge.

Designed by Daniel Libeskind, a Polish-Jewish architect based in the United States, the Jewish Museum is an exciting example of late 20th-century architecture. The plan, shape, style and interior and exterior arrangement of the building are all part of a philosophical concept to illustrate the history and culture of some 2,000 years of Germany's Jewish community and the repercussions of the Holocaust. The exhibition displays many artifacts, such as books and photographs, to paint a vivid picture of Jewish experiences. There is a special exhibition on the philosopher Moses Mendelssohn. The long, narrow galleries with slanting floors and sharp turns are designed to evoke the feeling of loss and dislocation. These are interspersed with "voids" that represent the vacuum left behind by the destruction of Jewish life.

Fractured styling on the exterior of Berlin's Jewish Museum

Daniel Libeskind's Design

The extraordinary zinc-clad, jagged structure of the main museum building is likened to a deconstructed Star of David. Across the road, in a converted flower market, is a new Libeskind-designed extension, the Jüdische Akademie. This houses research resources, archives and educational facilities. A quote by the medieval Jewish philosopher Moses Maimonides – "Hear the truth, whoever speaks it" – appears on the façade in five languages. The striking entrance hall has skylights shaped like the first letters of the Hebrew alphabet, Alef and Bet.

The striking, jagged structure of the Jewish Museum

Moses Mendelssohn's glasses, one of the museum's everyday objects

Moses Mendelssohn

One section, entitled "Moses Mendelssohn and the Enlightenment", details the fight of the poor Dessau-born philosopher (1729–86) for religious tolerance at a time when Jews possessed no civil rights.

Symbolic pillars in the Garden of Exile and Emigration

Everyday Life

One section of the museum is devoted to aspects of Jewish traditions, such as the observation of the Sabbath and the concept of kosher food. The changing role of the family as well as the position of Jews within society are also analysed.

A 16th-century rat-like charm, meant to dispel diseases

German and Jewish

In 1871 Jews attained equal rights in Germany. Attracted by the capital city, they were prominent figures in trade, industry and culture. Their role in society is typified by Emil Rathenau, who founded Germany's largest electrical company, AEG. The large department stores Wertheim and Tietz were founded by Jews, as was the publishing house Ullstein. Arnold Schönberg became famous for his revolutionary classical music, Max Reinhardt for his theatre productions, Walter Benjamin for his theory of modernity and Max Liebermann for his painting.

Persecution and Hope

German and Jewish soldiers fought side by side in the Great War, but anti-Jewish voices became louder. The prosecution of Jews is charted through to the genocide in the Third Reich and beyond.

The Garden of Exile and Emigration features 49 tilted pillars, each 6 m (20 ft) high. 48 of these, filled with Berlin earth, represent the founding of the state of Israel in 1948; the 49th, filled with earth from Jerusalem, represents the city of Berlin. The garden symbolizes the forced exile of Germany's Jews and the disorientation caused by emigration, while new growth at the top of the pillars stands for hope and peace.

Kadishman's Fallen Leaves shows 10,000 faces of Jewish victims

Martin-Gropius-Bau

Martin-Gropius-Bau ❷

Map G5. Niederkirchnerstrasse 7. Open Wed–Mon. Adm charge.

Originally built as an arts and crafts museum by Martin Gropius in 1881, this superb building was left in ruins after World War II. Finally rebuilt in 1981 and further refurbished in 1999, it now houses changing exhibitions on art, photography and architecture.

Topographie des Terrors ❸

Map G5. Stresemannstrasse 110 (entrance on Niederkirchner Strasse). Open daily. Free.

The block of buildings here that once housed three of Nazi Germany's most feared institutions – the security service, the Gestapo and the SS – was razed to the ground after the war. In 1987 the surviving cellars – former

Exhibits in Topographie des Terrors

torture cells – were used to mount an exhibition chronicling Nazi war crimes, and in 2010, the above-ground Documentation Center was added. A preserved section of the wall runs alongside.

Checkpoint Charlie ❹

Map G5. Haus am Checkpoint Charlie: Friedrichstrasse 43–45. Open daily. Adm charge.

During 1961–90, Checkpoint Charlie was the only crossing point for foreigners between East and West Berlin. Today you can see a replica checkpoint booth plus, in the nearby museum, Haus am Checkpoint Charlie, the story of the building of the wall and ways in which people tried to escape from the East.

Berlinische Galerie ❺

Map H5. Alte Jakobstrasse 124–8. Open Wed–Mon.

The museum for modern art, design and architecture has a huge collection of German, East European and Russian art. A highlight is the vast painting collection, covering all major art movements from the late 19th century to today. It includes works by Baselitz, Grosz and Kirchner.

Deutsches Technikmuseum Berlin ❻

Map G5. Trebbiner Strasse 9. Open Tue–Sun. Adm charge.

Founded in 1982, this museum showcases a wide range of locomotives and railway carriages as well as vintage cars and planes. The popular Spectrum area allows visitors a "hands-on" experience.

Friedhöfe vor dem Halleschen Tor **7**

Map G6. Mehringdamm, Blücher-, Baruther & Zossener Strasse. Open daily. Free.

Beyond the city walls, next to the Hallesches Tor, four neighbouring cemeteries were established in 1735. Some of Berlin's greatest artists are buried here, including the composer Mendelssohn-Bartholdy, architects von Knobelsdorff, Gilly and Langhans, and the writer, composer and composer E T A Hoffmann.

Riehmers Hofgarten **8**

Map G6. Yorckstrasse 83–6, Grossbeerenstrasse 56–7 & Hagelberger Strasse 9–12.

Over 20 buildings make up this elegant estate, built around a picturesque garden by Wilhelm Riehmer and Otto Mrosk as officers' quarters in 1871–92. Attractively restored, the area also includes a pleasant hotel with a restaurant.

Viktoriapark **9**

Map G6/7.

This rambling park, with water features, short trails and a small hill, was set up as a recreational space for workers in 1888–94 to plans by Hermann Mächtig. At the top is a 66-m- (216-ft-) high Neo-Gothic memorial, created by Schinkel in 1817–21. It commemorates the Prussian victory in the Wars of Liberation against Napoleon.

Renaissance-style façade in Riehmers Hofgarten

STREET LIFE

RESTAURANTS

Altes Zollhaus
Map H6. Carl-Herz-Ufer 30.
Tel 692 33 00. **Expensive**
Gourmet-style German food in a half-timbered house.

Defne
Map J6. Planufer 92c.
Tel 81 79 71 11. **Moderate**
Award-winning Turkish food.

Osteria No. 1
Map G6. Kreuzbergstrasse 71.
Tel 786 91 62. **Moderate**
Great Italian pasta and pizza.

BARS AND PUBS

Mister Hu
Map E6. Goltzstrasse 39.
Popular, relaxed cocktail bar.

SHOPPING

Bergmannstrasse
Map G6. Great for knick-knack and secondhand shops.

Türkenmarkt Maybachufer
Map J6. Maybachufer.
Open Tue & Fri.
Exotic Turkish street market.

See p80 for price codes.

AROUND KURFÜRSTENDAMM

First developed in the 19th century, the area around the glamorous Kurfürstendamm boulevard (or Ku'damm for short) underwent years of decline after 1945. Today it is fashionable once more, with great architecture, elegant boutiques and a lively street scene around Breitscheidplatz.

SIGHTS AT A GLANCE

Museums
Museum für Fotografie **6**

Streets and Squares
Fasanenstrasse **8**
Kurfürstendamm **4**
Savignyplatz **9**
Tauentzienstrasse **10**

Parks
Zoologischer Garten **1**

Historic Buildings
Europa-Center **2**
Jüdisches Gemeindehaus **7**
KaDeWe **11**
Kaiser-Wilhelm-Gedächtnis-kirche pp64–5 **3**
Ludwig-Erhard-Haus **5**

SEE ALSO

• *Street Life p67.*

KEY

🚉	Railway station
🇺	U-Bahn
Ⓢ	S-Bahn
🚌	Bus terminus

| 0 metres | 800 |
| 0 yards | 800 |

◀ A mosaic inside the Kaiser-Wilhelm-Gedächtniskirche

Zoologischer Garten ❶

Map D4/5. Hardenbergplatz 8 or Budapester Strasse 34. Open daily. Adm charge.

The Zoological Garden, part of the Tiergarten, dates from 1844. One of the best-stocked zoos in the world, it is filled with elaborate habitats such as the new 47-room aviary. There is also a monkey house, a nocturnal pavilion and a hippopotamus pool with a glazed wall to enable visitors to observe the occupants underwater. The aquarium, one of the largest in Europe, contains sharks, piranhas and coral reef fish. There is also a huge terrarium that houses a group of crocodiles.

Penguins, among some 18,000 animals in the Zoological Garden

Kaiser-Wilhelm-Gedächtniskirche ❸

See pp64–5.

Kurfürstendamm ❹

Map C/D5.

One of Berlin's most elegant streets, this wide avenue (the "Ku'damm") was established in the 1880s. Between World Wars I and II its legendary cafés, such as Café Kranzler, attracted writers, directors and artists. After World War II, damaged houses were replaced with modern ones. The symbol of consumerism and West Berlin's main shopping street during the Cold War, Ku'damm today boasts elegant shops and cafés.

Inside the Europa-Center

Europa-Center ❷

Map D5. Breitscheidplatz.

Helmut Hentrich and Hubert Petschnigg's Europa-Center, opened in 1962, contains a group of low-rise buildings with a shopping mall, restaurants and pubs, the de luxe Palace Hotel, and a 22-storey office block. The somewhat dated Center incorporates fountains, such as the "Flow of Time Clock", by Bernard Gitton. The Center is also home to the political cabaret Die Stachelschweine (the porcupines) and, in the tower, the Puro Sky Lounge.

The Kranzler Eck and Café Kranzler on Kurfürstendamm

The distinctive curve of Ludwig-Erhard-Haus

Ludwig-Erhard-Haus ⑤

Map C5. Fasanenstrasse 83–4. Open Mon–Fri.

This innovative building houses the headquarters of the Berlin stock exchange. Designed by Nicholas Grimshaw and completed in 1998, it has been compared to an armadillo, a skeleton and a shell. The main structure comprises 15 elliptical arches, which extend above the roof and down through the glass walls on each side of the building.

Museum für Fotografie ⑥

Map D4. Jebensstrasse 2. Open Tue–Sun. Adm charge.

After his death in 2004, the society and art photographer Helmut Newton left his life's work to the city of Berlin. Newton, who was born and trained as a photographer in Berlin, became one of the 20th century's most famous photographers. The museum plans to broaden its collections to eventually serve as the city's main museum of photography. Exhibitions include Newton's fashion and nude photography, self-portraits and landscapes.

Jüdisches Gemeindehaus ⑦

Map C5. Fasanenstrasse 79–80.

The Jewish community has its headquarters in this building, constructed on the site of a synagogue that was burned down on Kristallnacht, 9 November 1938. The original synagogue was designed by Hessel in a Romanesque-Byzantine style and built in 1912. The ruins were removed only in the mid-1950s. The new building, designed by Knoblauch and Heise, was constructed in 1959. The only reminders of the splendour of the former synagogue are the portal and some decorative fragments on the façade. Inside there are offices, a school, a kosher restaurant and a prayer room covered by three glazed domes. At the rear there is a courtyard with a place of remembrance. A statue at the front of the building depicts a broken scroll of the Torah.

Jüdisches Gemeindehaus entrance

Kaiser-Wilhelm-Gedächtniskirche ❸

The Neo-Romanesque church was given its present
name in 1895, to honour Wilhelm I. Following
severe bomb damage in 1943, the ruins of the
tower were left standing as a memorial. Next to it,
Egon Eiermann built a new church in 1957–63.

The Kaiser's Mosaic
*depicts Kaiser Heinrich I,
sitting on his throne.*

Original mosaics
*featuring the dukes
of Prussia can be
seen on the arches
and the walls near
the staircase.*

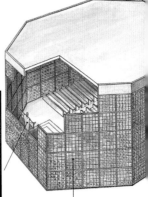

The Main Altar *is
dominated by a vast
figure of Christ on the
Cross by Karl Hemmeter.*

*Walls of reinforced
concrete and blue-
coloured glass
form a dense grid.*

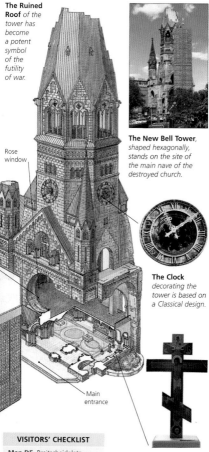

The Ruined Roof of the tower has become a potent symbol of the futility of war.

The New Bell Tower, shaped hexagonally, stands on the site of the main nave of the destroyed church.

Rose window

The Clock decorating the tower is based on a Classical design.

Main entrance

The Orthodox Cross was donated by the Russian Orthodox bishops of Yuryev and Volokolamsk, in memory of the victims of Nazism.

VISITORS' CHECKLIST

Map D5. Breitscheidplatz. Church open to visitors daily except during services. Free. Gedenkhalle open Mon–Sat. Free. **www. gedaechtniskirche-berlin.de**

Fasanenstrasse – one of the most elegant streets in Berlin

Fasanenstrasse 8

Map C5/6.

On Fasanenstrasse, well-maintained buildings, *fin-de-siècle* villas, elegant jewellers', art galleries and exclusive designer shops all make for a pleasant afternoon's stroll. The villas at Nos. 23–5, called Wintergarten-Ensemble, are worth seeing. No. 23 houses the Literaturhaus, which organizes exhibitions and readings and has a café. At No. 24 is the Käthe-Kollwitz-Museum, and at No. 25, built in 1892 by Grisebach, is an auction house and art gallery.

Savignyplatz 9

Map C5.

Savignyplatz is enclosed on the south side by the arcade of a railway viaduct, which appears in the film *Cabaret*. During the day the square does not look interesting but it comes alive at night. The cafés and restaurants fill up, and in summer the edge of the square and neighbouring streets turn into one large garden filled with tables and umbrellas. People come from outlying districts to visit popular restaurants. Cafés and bars are located in the arcades in the viaduct.

Tauentzienstrasse 10

Map D5.

One of the most important streets for trade and commerce in this part of the city; the shops are not as exclusive as those on Ku'damm, but attract more visitors. One of the highlights of the street is the unusual façade of the Peek & Cloppenburg department store, designed by Böhm. Other attractions are the central flowerbed and a sculpture by Brigitte and Martin Matschinsky-Denninghoff, erected in 1987 on the 750th anniversary of Berlin.

KaDeWe 11

Map D5. Tauentzienstrasse 21–4. Open Mon–Sat.

Kaufhaus des Westens (the west's department store) is continental Europe's largest department store, built in 1907 by Emil Schaudt. You can buy everything here, but its main attraction is as a gourmet's paradise, with the largest collection of foodstuffs in the whole of Europe and numerous in-store food bars where you can sample the produce on the spot.

Balconies on Savignyplatz

STREET LIFE

RESTAURANTS

Austeria Brasserie
Map C5. Kurfürstendamm 184.
Tel 881 84 61. **Moderate**
Popular eatery, specializing in
oysters, lobster and fish.

Dressler
Map C5. Kurfürstendamm
207–8. Tel 883 35 30.
Moderate
Genuine French brasserie
atmosphere and food.

First Floor (Palace Hotel)
Map C5. Budapester Strasse
45. Tel 25 02 10 20. **Expensive**
Michelin-starred, high-quality
German fare, celebrity chef.

Lubitsch
Map C5. Bleibtreustrasse 47.
Tel 882 37 56. **Moderate**
Good-value German and inter-
national cuisine, lively setting.

Paris Bar
Map C5. Kantstrasse 152.
Tel 313 80 52. **Expensive**
Exclusive French bistro, haunt
of artists and politicians.

BARS AND PUBS

Bar am Lützowplatz
Map E5. Lützowplatz 7.
Former haunt of "the beautiful people", boasts longest bar
in Berlin, barmen in formal
dress, outstanding cocktails.

Dicke Wirtin
Map C5. Carmerstrasse 9.
"The fat landlady" is a traditional Berlin Kneipe (pub)
which also serves hearty food.

Times Bar
Map C5. Fasanenstrasse 9.
Some of the best cocktails in
town are served at this stylish
bar in the Savoy Hotel.

Trompete
Map E5. Lützowplatz 9.
Very trendy but comfortable
bar. Live concerts at weekends
(all types of music from jazz
and salsa to house).

Wiener Beisl
Map D5. Kantstrasse 152.
Adjoining the Paris Bar, serves
Austrian cuisine.

CAFÉS

Café Einstein
Map E5. Kurfürstenstrasse 58.
A Berlin landmark in an
elegant villa, once owned by
a movie star, serving delicious
cakes and coffees from their
own roasting room.

Café Wintergarten
Map C5. Fasanenstrasse 23.
Beautiful setting, in an old
townhouse's conservatory.

Confiserie Leysieffer
Map C5. Kurfürstendamm 218.
One of Berlin's oldest patisse-
ries, in a former embassy.

SHOPPING

ART 1900
Map C5. Kurfürstendamm 53.
Antiques shop with a variety
of Art Nouveau trinkets.

Mientus
Map C5. Kurfürstendamm 52.
Fashion from top designers
such as Gucci, Prada and
Dolce & Gabbana.

Stilwerk
Map C5. Kantstrasse 17.
Shopping centre specializing
in designer furnishings.

See p80 for price codes.

CHARLOTTENBURG

The Charlottenburg area gained status when Elector Friedrich III (later King Friedrich I) built the Schloss, his wife's summer retreat, here in the late 1600s. A wealthy, independent district, it only became part of Berlin in 1920. Despite World War II and the division of the city, the area has kept its historic character – urbane and elegant.

SIGHTS AT A GLANCE

Museums
Bröhan-Museum ⑩
Neuer Flügel ③
Sammlung Berggruen ⑨
Sammlung Scharf-
Gerstenberg ⑤

Historic Buildings
Belvedere ⑧
Luisenkirche ⑫
Mausoleum ⑦

Neuer Pavillon ④
Schloss Charlottenburg ①
Schlossstrasse Villas ⑪

Parks and Gardens
Schlosspark ⑥

Monuments
Reiterdenkmal des Grossen
Kurfürsten ②

SEE ALSO

• Street Life p73.

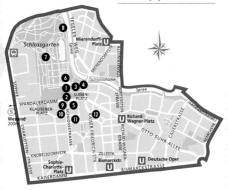

KEY

🚌 Bus terminus

Ⓤ U-Bahn

Ⓢ S-Bahn

| 0 metres | 800 |
| 0 yards | 800 |

◄ The glorious main façade of Schloss Charlottenburg

The central, and oldest, section of Schloss Charlottenburg

Schloss Charlottenburg ❶

Map A3. Spandauer Damm. Open Tue–Sun. Adm charge.

The palace in Charlottenburg was intended as a summer home for Sophie Charlotte, Elector Friedrich III's wife. Construction began in 1695 to a design by Johann Arnold Nering. Between 1701 and 1713 Johann Friedrich Eosander enlarged the palace, crowning it with a cupola and adding the orangery wing. Subsequent extensions were undertaken by Frederick the Great (Friedrich II), who had two apartments furnished for himself in the palace. Taking a personal interest in the design, he added the Neuer Flügel, by Georg Wenzeslaus von Knobelsdorff, between 1740 and 1746. Restored to its former elegance following World War II, its collection of richly decorated interiors is unequalled in Berlin.

Reiterdenkmal des Grossen Kurfürsten ❷

Map A3. Luisenplatz.

The equestrian statue of the Great Elector (Friedrich Wilhelm) is among his finest portraits. It was created in 1696–1703 to a design by Schlüter. Moved to safety during World War II, it was lost when the barge moving it sank at Tegel. In 1949 the statue was retrieved from the water and erected in the courtyard of Schloss Charlottenburg. The original base, which was left in East Berlin, was replaced by a copy.

Statue of the Great Elector

Neuer Flügel ❸

Map A3. Luisenplatz. Open Tue–Sun. Adm charge.

The two-storey New Wing was added by Frederick the Great in 1740, to designs by Knobelsdorff. In the king's residence two magnificent rooms can be seen, Goldene Galerie and Weisser Saal (white room), containing his fine collection of paintings by Watteau and others, as well as exquisite furniture.

Neuer Pavillon (Schinkel-Pavillon) **4**

Map B3. Luisenplatz (Schlosspark Charlottenburg). Open Tue–Sun. Adm charge.

This charming Neo-Classical pavilion was built in 1825 by Schinkel for Friedrich Wilhelm III and his second wife. The two-storey structure has a central staircase, pillared galleries and a cast iron balcony. Inside the pavilion are period interiors, pictures and sculptures. Also displayed are paintings from the old Galerie der Romantik, including Casper David Friedrich landscapes and works by Schinkel himself.

The Neuer Pavillon, modelled on the Villa Reale del Chiamonte, Italy

Sammlung Scharf-Gerstenberg **5**

Map A3. Schlossstrasse 70. Open Tue–Sun. Adm charge.

Located opposite Schloss Charlottenburg, the Scharf-Gerstenberg Collection exhibits outstanding works by the Surrealists and their forerunners, including Piranesi, Redon, Goya, Dalí, Magritte, Paul Klee, Max Ernst and Dubuffet. A film programme includes classic Surrealist films by Luis Buñel and Salvador Dalí.

Schlosspark **6**

Map A3. Luisenplatz (Schloss Charlottenburg). Free.

The large royal park around Schloss Charlottenburg was largely rebuilt after World War II, when 18th-century prints were used as reference. Behind the palace is a French-style Baroque garden, with strict geometric designs, trimmed shrubs and ornate fountains. Farther away, beyond the carp pond, is a less formal English-style landscaped park, designed by Lenné in 1819–28.

Mausoleum **7**

Map A3. Luisenplatz (Schlosspark Charlottenburg). Open Tue–Sun. Adm charge.

Queen Luise, beloved wife of Friedrich Wilhelm III, was laid to rest in this modest mausoleum by Schinkel. After the king's death in 1840, the mausoleum was refurbished and the queen's tomb was moved to one side, leaving room for her husband's tomb. The king's second wife and, later, Kaiser Wilhelm I and his wife were also buried in the crypt.

Mausoleum

The Belvedere, designed by Langhans

Belvedere ⑧

Map A2. Spandauer Damm (Schlosspark Charlottenburg). Open Tue–Sun. Adm charge.

The Belvedere summer-house in the Schlosspark served as a tea pavilion for Friedrich Wilhelm II. It was also used as a watchtower in times of war. Dating from 1788, it was designed by C G Langhans to include both Baroque and Neo-Classical elements. The oval central building has four straight-sided annexes. It is crowned by a dome with a sculpture of cherubs and a basket of flowers. Ruined during World War II, the summer-house was reconstructed in 1956–60. It now houses a large collection of porcelain from the Berlin Königliche Porzellan-Manufaktur (Royal Porcelain Factory).

Sammlung Berggruen ⑨

Map A3. Schlossstrasse 1. Open Tue–Sun. Adm charge.

The gallery, opened in 1996, displays Heinz Berggruen's art collection from the late 1800s and is famous for its Picasso paintings, drawings and gouaches. Other highlights include works by Paul Klee and fine sculptures by Laurens and Giacometti.

Bröhan-Museum ⑩

Map A3. Schlossstrasse 1a. Open Tue–Sun. Adm charge.

This small museum displays Karl H Bröhan's collection, amassed since 1966, of Art Nouveau and Art Deco works. It features Berlin Secession-ists such as Hagemeister and Baluschek, plus furniture, ceramics, glassware, silverwork and textiles.

Schlossstrasse Villas ⓫

Map A4. Schlossstrasse 65–7.

Most of the historic villas that once graced Schloss-strasse no longer exist. However, a few were carefully restored. No. 65, No. 66 and especially No. 67 are noteworthy. No. 67 was built in 1873, in a Neo-Classical style to a design by G Töbelmann. After World War II, the building was returned to its former splendour. The front garden, a characteristic of the area, was restored in 1986. Nearby, the rich local art collection of Museum Charlottenburg-Wilmersdorf is housed in the Neo-Renaissance Villa Oppenheim at no. 55.

Luisenkirche ⓬

Map B4. Gierkeplatz.
Open Mon–Fri. Free.

This small church, designed by Martin Böhme from plans by Philipp Gerlach, was built in 1713–16. Its Baroque styling was removed in the next course of rebuilding, by Schinkel in 1823–6, when it was renamed after Queen Luise. The church underwent further refurbishment after it was damaged during World War II. The shape of the church is based on a traditional Greek cross, with a tower at the front. The interior fixtures and fittings are not original, and the elegant stained-glass windows date from 1956.

Front-door decoration on a villa in Charlottenburg

STREET LIFE

RESTAURANTS

Ana e Bruno
Map A4. Sophie-Charlotten-Strasse 101. Tel 325 71 10.
Expensive
Top-class Italian restaurant, well-known beyond the area.

Ratskeller Charlottenburg
Map A4. Otto-Suhr-Allee 102.
Tel 341 89 09. **Moderate**
Excellent German and international food with seasonal specialities served in the atmospheric town hall cellars.

CAFÉS

Kleine Orangerie
Map A3. Schloss Charlottenburg.
Spandauer Damm 20.
Breakfasts, snacks, lunches, afternoon teas and light meals in the palace orangery.

SHOPPING

Gipsformerei
Map A3. Sophie-Charlotten-Strasse 17.
Workshop selling replicas of famous museum exhibits.

See p80 for price codes.

Survival Guide

As with all major European cities, mind your wallet, particularly on public transport during rush hours. If you run into trouble or need advice, the police will help – often they speak English. For minor health problems, a pharmacist can sort you out.

MONEY

Currency

German currency is the euro. Bank notes come as 5 (grey), 10 (pink), 20 (blue), 50 (orange), 100 (green), 200 (yellow) and 500 euros (purple). Coins are 2 and 1 euros (silver and gold); 50, 20 and 10 cents (gold); and 5, 2 and 1 cents (bronze).

Banks

You can bring any amount of cash, but credit or debit cards are safer. Rates of exchange vary; check also for any commission charge. Banks are usually open 9am–6pm Mon–Fri.

Changing money

Bureaux de Change (*Wechselstuben*) are often found near train stations, such as the Hauptbahnhof and Zoo Station. Hotel reception desks often exchange cash, but their rates can be poor.

Credit cards

Many stores and restaurants in Berlin do not accept credit cards, while some

Cash machine in Berlin

outlets require a minimum purchase; always check before buying.

COMMUNICATIONS

Internet

Internet centres are common throughout Berlin. Rates can vary greatly, so check before using a terminal. Berlin is trialling free public Wi-Fi access in parts of the city centre. Expect to find it in many cafés and libraries.

Postal Services

German post offices have yellow Deutsche Post signs. Postboxes are also yellow. You can send registered letters, parcels and money orders from the post office, where you can also buy stamps and telephone cards.

A typical postbox

Telephones

Coin-operated telephones are less common than card-operated ones. Telephone cards are sold at all post offices, as well as department stores and kiosks. Some public phones accept credit cards – you just place your credit card in the phone and tap in your PIN.

Symbol for pharmacy

HEALTH

Emergency Treatment
EU citizens should take their European Health Insurance Card to cover emergency treatment. Non-EU visitors should buy special health insurance. If sudden illness strikes, you can call an ambulance (tel 112), but if the state of the patient allows, drive them to the nearest Emergency Room.

Minor Ailments
If the complaint is minor, a chemist (*Apotheke*) can help. When closed, they display the addresses of pharmacies that are open.

Helplines
Helpful telephone lines include Narcotics Emergencies (192 37), Help-line International (44 01 06 07, 6pm–midnight) and the Emergency Doctor (31 00 31, 24 hours). Your embassy should also be able to provide a list of doctors who speak your language.

Street stamp-vending machine

SAFETY

Theft
Keep valuables in a hotel safe. Major theft is rare, but pickpockets are active, particularly on the U-Bahn.

Railway Stations
Stations are often patrolled by guards, especially after dark – ask them if you need help. Panic buttons are installed on each platform.

Insurance
Before you travel, buy insurance. If you experience street crime, report it to the police immediately and obtain a statement confirming what was stolen.

Fire
If there's a fire, phone the Fire Brigade (*Feuerwehr*, tel 112), or use a bright-red public fire alarm.

Police officers

EMERGENCY NUMBERS

Police 110 **Ambulance** 112.
Emergency dentist
Tel 89 00 43 33 (recorded message in German).
Emergency doctor
Tel 31 00 31 or 116 117.
Emergency pharmacy
Tel 31 00 31.
Credit card cancellation
Tel 116 116.

Getting Around

Much of the city centre can easily be seen on foot, but for areas further afield, use public transport. Buses, trams, U-Bahn or S-Bahn will quickly get you anywhere, and special cycling lanes also make it easy to explore Berlin by bicycle.

A typical double-decker bus

Buses and Trams

Travelling by **bus** can be trying in the rush hour, but it is fine at other times. Most major roads have bus lanes so buses are punctual even in heavy traffic. A double-decker bus is worth taking for a good view of the sights from the top deck.

Modern tram, operating in the former East Berlin

Trams operate mainly within former East Berlin; only one route was extended to Wedding in the north. Trams are punctual as they never get stuck in traffic.

Stops for trams and buses are marked with an H (*Halte-stelle*). They display the appropriate numbers, timetables and route maps.

U-Bahn and S-Bahn

There are two local train services in Berlin: the (mainly) underground U-Bahn and the (mainly) overground suburban commuter S-Bahn trains.

The **U-bahn** network is one of the

Bus stop

best in Europe, with ten lines serving all of central Berlin. There are many stations at short distances from each other, and during rush hours trains arrive every minute or so. Even at other times, the U-Bahn is a fast and efficient service. Its lines operate 4am–12:30am Sun–Thu and 24 hours on weekends.

The **S-Bahn** train routes extend far beyond the confines of the centre, serving Berlin's suburbs. There are 17 S-Bahn lines in total, of which five run along the main central axis from West- to Ostkreuz. The stations are spaced further apart than U-Bahn stops, and trains run every 10 or 20 minutes. S-Bahn trains are a useful alternative in the centre and a must for exploring Berlin's outer districts.

Tickets

Berlin has an integrated transport system and tickets are valid for S- and U-Bahn trains as well as buses and trams. The city has three travel zones. Most sights in this book fall within Zone A. You can buy tickets for combinations of zones.

Single tickets come at two prices: normal (*Normaltarif*) and short-trip (*Kurzstrecke*). The former is valid for a single journey on all public transport, with as many changes as you need, while the latter can only be used for three stops on trains and six on buses.

A tourist boat on the Spree river

Boats

A relaxing three- or four-hour boat journey will take you past many sights. Go along the Spree river and the Landwehrkanal to admire historic Mitte as the boat passes the Berliner Dom along Museum Island. Head off to the government district and the Reichstag, then pass the Haus der Kulturen der Welt before entering the Landwehr-kanal. This runs past the Zoological Garden and buildings on Potsdamer Platz, and passes through Kreuzberg on its way to the junction with the Spree at Oberbaumbrücke.

Tickets

Machines and ticket counters at station entrances sell single tickets, returns, and 1-, 3- and 7-day travel cards. Bus drivers only sell single tickets. You must validate your ticket before travelling by punching it into a machine (*Entwerter*) found on train platforms or in buses. Plain-clothes inspectors frequently check that you have a valid ticket.

TRAVEL INFORMATION

BVG Information (public transport) Tel 194 49; www.bvg.de

Ticket Information S-Bahn Bahnhof Alexanderplatz, Tel 27 74 33 33.

S-Bahn Service Centre Friedrichstrasse, Georgenstrasse 14, Tel 29 74 33 33.

U-Bahn Service Centre U-Bahnhof Turmstrasse, 6:30am–8pm Mon–Fri.

BVG Lost Property U-Bahn Kleiststrasse, Tel 194 49.

Taxis Tel 261 026; 210 101; 44 33 22; 20 20 20.

An S-Bahn train, line S5

Index